SCOUT, the Christmas Dog

SCOUT,
the Christmas Dog

BY ANDREW SANSOM

with illustrations by
Clemente Guzman III

TEXAS A&M UNIVERSITY PRESS   COLLEGE STATION

TO ALEXANDER

May you have the great gifts of good friends and good dogs

Copyright © 2006 by Andrew Sansom
Manufactured in China
First edition

LIBRARY OF CONGRESS
CATALOGING-IN-PUBLICATION DATA

Sansom, Andrew.
Scout, the Christmas dog / by Andrew Sansom ;
with illustrations by Clemente Guzman III.
p. cm.
ISBN-13: 978-1-58544-562-2 (cloth : alk. paper)
ISBN-10: 1-58544-562-2 (cloth : alk. paper)
1. Labrador retriever—Texas—Biography. 2. Bird dogs—
Texas—Biography. 3. Fowling—Texas. 4. Sansom, Andrew.
I. Title.
SF429.L3S26 2006
636.752'7—dc22
2006011666

The drawing on p. 32 is based on a photograph
by Mark Matson for the Austin *American Statesman*

I grew up on the Texas coast, just inside a line of trees separating us from the vast swath of coastal prairies and marshes that bring millions of migrating waterfowl each year from as far away as Russia and the Canadian Arctic. I marked my birthday each autumn by the sound of geese flying in at night high above the fog, and I scheduled my life around hunting them.

A typical hunt would begin before daylight at the old Palmer's Sporting Goods Store on the way to a place we called the Slop Bowl. There the hunters would gather for the latest tall tales, last-minute purchases, and occasionally some good information. The owner's son was my friend and companion, Corky Palmer, who was also my mentor where hunting was concerned. Corky's legendary dog, Boomer, usually kept us up half the night in his excitement to get to the field.

One of Texas' most historic waterfowl hunting areas, the Slop Bowl is aptly named. Lying just inside the intracoastal canal near the mouth of the Brazos River where Stephen F. Austin's first boatload of colonists washed up after a shipwreck, the brackish Slop Bowl is one of the wildest marshes left on the Texas coast. Hundreds of small potholes dapple the vast, saline grassland like sequins on a deep green quilt. Navigating the Slop Bowl is a formidable challenge; vehicles routinely get stuck up to the axles, and hunters bog down to their knees in the muck.

We had wonderful times together in those days at the Slop Bowl, telling the same old jokes, watching the birds streaking into the dawn, and enjoying Boomer's determination to play his special role to its fullest. From Boomer, I came to appreciate the dignity and courage of Labrador retrievers, and in the heavy atmosphere of tradition and lasting relationships, we all formed a bond of hunters and dogs that has lasted most of our lifetimes. Corky's rapport with Boomer so indelibly marked me that when I had Labs of my own, I strove to emulate my friend's dedication to his dog and to capture for myself a semblance of their strong connection.

Every year, Corky and I still look forward to getting back to the marshes and rice, to welcome the birds back to Texas, and to celebrate the noble canines that accompany us and do the hardest part of the job. Thus it was a devastating blow when, while hunting with Corky one late December, I lost my dog, Scout—my other best friend.

Scout came to me at Christmas more than twelve years ago. At the time we had an old standard poodle my daughter named Sasquatch because of his huge puppy feet. He was fourteen years old and had gone deaf and blind. He was pretty incontinent, and whenever he did decide to go outside, I had to help him up off the floor. Very reluctantly, and I have to say belatedly, we had decided to put old Sasquatch to sleep. But it was Christmastime, and we decided to wait until after the holidays before we said goodbye to him for the last time.

On Christmas Day, our family was gathered around the tree, opening presents. Sasquatch was curled up asleep in his favorite spot in front of the fire. Knowing how sad his impending departure was for me, Nona—my wife, mistress of the perfect surprise—presented me with a little box containing a card that said I had not one but two new Labrador puppies waiting for me to pick up as soon as they were weaned. As sad as losing Sasquatch was at the time, the anticipation of having, for the first time in my life, a couple of dogs that could hunt with me was as thoughtful and exciting a Christmas gift as anyone has ever given me. The season was bittersweet: a great loss and a new beginning.

Several days after the presents had all been opened and the turkey leftovers had all been eaten, Nona, my daughter April, and I sat down in front of the fire with Sasquatch for the last time. He loved that fire, I think mainly because it warmed his old joints and its location was a central vantage point where he could at least sense what was going on in the house, especially the presence of his family. Sasquatch had been with us for a long time and through our most tumultuous period. He grew up with our children and accompanied them for hours as they ranged through the woodlands next to our home on the Texas coast. I had hoped that he would be a retriever, but he had little interest in bringing things back to me and absolutely hated the water. He was, however, an incredible snake dog and would continuously circle the kids as they walked through the woods, keeping them safe from any snakes that might come their way. When he caught one, he would take the snake in his mouth and violently shake it until it was dead. I have no idea where he developed this skill or what genetic makeup predisposed him to such behavior, but in the swampy bottomlands where we lived, it was a great and welcome attribute for a family dog.

The other thing about Sasquatch was that he was incredibly smart. I taught that old dog new tricks when he was so frail he could hardly get around, but he never seemed to get too old to learn new ways to please me. He was so eager to do so, in fact, that sometimes when I instructed him to do something basic, like sit or speak, he would go through his entire repertoire of tricks all at once, rolling over, heeling, smiling, and all the rest just to get the preliminaries out of the way and go straight to the treat or the scratch behind his ears.

I was scratching him behind the ears in front of the fire when the vet came to our house and gave him the shot that created our last fulfilling experience with him. He drifted off to sleep in our laps, as he had done a thousand times, and we cried and cried as he faded away with the embers that had warmed us all.

After he was gone, I went to see my new Christmas puppies. Their mother was a white Lab and their father was chocolate, but all nine in the litter were jet black. They hardly had their eyes open when I first saw them, but I visited them frequently while they grew stronger, and I grew more grateful for the wonderful gift I had received.

The problem was that there were nine of them and I could take only two home with me. The books all say you need to take your new pup from its mother on the forty-ninth day for maximum bonding, so wanting to do this just right, I had a deadline for choosing. There were eight females in the bunch and only one male. I picked what seemed to be the liveliest and smartest female and the sole male and took them home with me on day forty-nine.

Everyone showed up for the arrival of the dogs. Corky came by to lend his dog wisdom. Our son, Andrew, and his wife, Petra, lived near us at the time,

and they were there along with April, Nona, and me. We dedicated a room in our house to the little guys and quickly began to appreciate the incredible capacity of Labrador puppies to destroy everything in sight.

It was unbelievable.

Those two tiny puppies, the picture of innocence, ate boots, ties, and even glass Christmas balls off the tree, which was still up. They chewed up the windowsills, ate through the gypsum board, and pulled the insulation right out of the walls. When they were old enough to be left outside for a while, they ate whole garden hoses. Years later, I would still occasionally find little pieces of green hose in the yard where they had passed through the extraordinary digestive tracts of my two Christmas dogs.

While we were starting to question whether the two pups were really a welcome addition to the family or the biggest mistake of our lives, we began the process of naming them.

Naming one dog is fairly simple but naming two presented us with both a challenge and a source of endless enjoyment. You can get books on naming dogs—and we did. We went through every conceivable combination of paired names at every family meal for days while the dogs chewed away at the house. On and on it went: Fire and Rain, MacNeil and Lehrer, Abu and Garcia, Desi and Luci, George and Gracie . . . . We perused our library for ideas and one evening pulled out an old copy of *To Kill a Mockingbird*. Suddenly, there was no question but that our quick, spirited little female was indeed a "Scout." The male was another matter.

He was just the opposite of Scout. She was constantly eager and ready to go; he took his time. She was bright and alert; he seemed aloof and even in a fog, wrapped up in his own world. She would come instantly when you called her; he took his time. She was small, and even at that stage we could tell he was going to be a big dog. We considered "Jem," Scout's brother in the book, and "Boo," the name of the strange man next door who saved Scout's life, but neither seemed to fit, though "Boo" was close. I remembered Corky's black Lab, Boomer, with whom he hunted almost every day during the season back down in the Slop Bowl. Boomer got so old that he couldn't handle the work any more, so Corky would take him out to the marshes, open up the back of the car, and sit with him while they watched the geese come in and listened to the elegiac sound of their cries in the air. In honor of that great dog, Scout's brother became Boomer, and all his life he reminded me of the relationship my friend had had with his dog.

I never respected Scout and Boomer more than in training. These dogs were literally born to bring things back to me. They were also born to swim. I discovered their spectacular natural attributes in this regard out in the Texas Hill Country near Stonewall on a lovely lake owned by my friend Terry Hershey from Houston, a non-hunter but one of the world's greatest lovers of dogs.

Boomer and Scout had been retrieving things since they were a few weeks old, but they had never been in the water until we started working together out at the Hershey ranch. The first time I threw their training dummy into the water, you would have thought they had been swimming all their lives; they looked as comfortable in water as they did on land.

When we began training at the lake, Boomer and Scout, who had literally never been apart, were so bonded to each other that they always jumped into the water at the same time, and I could not separate them.

I was faced with the challenge of teaching them to honor each other because during a hunt, only one dog at a time is sent out into the water for the prize. The many hours of work and the extreme patience it took all three of us to get one dog to sit on the shore while the other retrieved produced more satisfaction for me than almost anything else I can think of.

The differences in their personalities

really came out in those many hours together on the lake. When I threw her dummy out into the water and instructed her to fetch it, Scout would launch herself from shore like a rocket and seemingly leap most of the way to her objective. She sat quivering and vocalizing at my feet, anticipating her next turn to retrieve. Boomer, on the other hand, acted a lot of the time as if he could hardly care less. He had the instinct, for sure, but when the dummy was thrown, he would kind of tiptoe down to the water and put one paw in as if to test it before committing himself. Sometimes, while doing this, he would look up over his shoulder at me as if to say "Who me, boss? You want me to go out there?" But then he would go because it was in his genes, because he knew I wanted him to, and because deep down inside him somewhere he must have loved it as much as Scout did.

During those treasured times on the lake at Stonewall, I came to know that to really appreciate dogs is to experience and understand their intensity and sheer elation in doing what they are born to do, and to realize how our relationship with them can enhance their performance and their lives.

To my great dismay, however, I also discovered that my big-hearted Scout had somehow developed a fear of loud noises. That dog would walk through fire on my command and occasionally injure herself when relentlessly pursuing her objective, but a thunderstorm would bring her up in the bed with us at home, and while gunfire would not stop her from going after her training dummy, she would avoid bringing it back to me for fear I would shoot again. Though we both worked very hard on it for years, I never fully solved the problem, and because of it Scout and I never hunted together. Even so, we never stopped training, and we worked hard to overcome Scout's uncertainty around loud noises, as I learned from her how lucky we humans are to share a dog's joy in the field and be the recipients of such unqualified love.

We tried to make up for the lack of actual hunting experiences at Redbud Isle in Austin. Redbud Isle was formed in the Colorado River early in the last century in a flood so powerful that it destroyed the old dam that created what is now Lake Austin. Lying below the rebuilt Tom Miller Dam and formed with huge chunks of the rubble from the original structure, Redbud Isle was for many years an urban wilderness in the midst of one of the fastest growing cities in America—a perfect place for Boomer, Scout, and me. The island is only a few minutes from our house in travel time, but in other ways might as well be on the other side of the world. Lined with ancient cypress trees and lying beneath majestic limestone ramparts along Town Lake in Austin, the little island was a true escape from city life in the middle of town and a refuge for the dogs and me.

We went to Redbud Isle whenever we could. My respect for Boomer and Scout increased every time we were there together. It amazed me how the dogs enjoyed the river the most when it was running the swiftest. I could throw a dummy out into the current and they would actually lead it, swimming downstream and across the lake at the same time, intersecting their objective at precisely the right point to nab it and return to shore. Scout's unbelievable tenacity showed up when the flow was the strongest. I stupidly sent her out in the current one time when it was so strong that it swept her down stream and out of sight. I panicked and ran along the shore after her, finally catching up with her far downstream as she crawled up through the rocks onto the shore with the dummy in her mouth.

It also amazed me how much they enjoyed working in the cold. I could take them to Redbud Isle in twenty-degree weather, and they seemed to be even more invigorated than usual. They reminded me of seals with their thick, shiny black coats that shed all over the place in warm weather but also allowed them to do their thing in the lake even when there was ice on the water.

We occasionally ran into trouble at Redbud Isle. I remember one time I sent Scout out into the lake and she got tangled up in some fishing line that someone had thoughtlessly left in the water. I had to go in after her and free her so that she could swim back to shore. The island was neglected; that was one of the things that made it so wild, unique, and special for us, but also produced plenty of problems. In many ways, Redbud Isle was a mess. People dumped stuff there, and we were always having to negotiate around trash and other unpleasant reminders that the urban environment was still all too close.

I actually got motivated to change the conditions on the island and became part of a movement to encourage the city and the Lower Colorado River Authority to do something about it. Today, Redbud Isle is a different place. There is a paved parking lot with trash cans and well-established trails.

It is an official dog park, which means you can take your dogs there and free them from the leash. It is still extraordinarily beautiful and the trash is mostly gone, but the wildness is mostly gone as well. It can get overcrowded on the weekends with all the cars and people and dogs. We still go there to swim, because in spite of the blessings and curses of progress that have come to Redbud Isle, it remains our place.

Through the years, the three of us grew older together. Although Boomer and Scout did not hunt with me, they accompanied me almost everywhere else. If we were not at Redbud Isle, we were back out at the ranch in Stonewall where I would go to write.

Out of respect for our host's attitude toward hunting and because of Scout's fear of the gun, I never fired a shot at the ranch. Still, we found plenty of other adventures to keep us occupied. We took long walks together in the Hill Country, swam in the lake, and chased armadillos and other wild critters. When we couldn't be outdoors, I took them to work with me, and they became fixtures in the office.

At home, I taught them to get me the newspaper every morning. They enjoyed it so much that, for many years, they came back with six or seven papers and I had to develop a regular route on my way to work to get them back to their rightful owners.

Boomer got hit by a car one year, which caused him to have seizures that were excruciating to watch but never seemed to do him any permanent harm. He tore a ligament in his leg and had to have ACL surgery (an injury I always thought you got from skiing). The vet made him wear an Elizabethan collar for a few weeks to keep him from pulling his stitches out, and he was continually running into the walls and furniture with it. He weighed almost twice as much as Scout, and perhaps because of his size or his injuries, he seemed to age faster than she did, although she developed much more gray in her coat. I'll never forget the day I took them for a walk in the neighborhood on a summer day and Boomer was overcome by the heat. By the time we got back to the house, he was staggering and having trouble catching his breath. I laid him down and sprayed water on him with the garden hose. He eventually recovered, though the episode scared me to death.

The two of them remained inseparable. It was as if they were one organism. From their earliest days, Scout, who was entirely devoted to Boomer, developed a curious habit of chewing on his ear. She would take his entire ear in her mouth and gently gnaw on it for hours. He seemed to love it, and this endured as the most obvious manifestation of the near-umbilical connection between the two of them.

Over the years, I tried many ways to keep them contained while I was gone during the day—most were failures. We had an electric fence for a while, but Boomer was immune to the shocks. I built a regular wire fence, and Scout climbed over it like it wasn't there. I finally built a kennel for them in the backyard, and that's where they spent most of their time when I wasn't with them. Each day when I came home from work, they recognized the sound of my car, and I watched them jump to their feet in anticipation as I pulled into the driveway. This afternoon homecoming became another of our shared rituals, and no matter how long I stayed away or how late I was in coming home, they were always glad to see me.

One day I got home from work at the regular time and noticed as I passed the kennel that Boomer did not get up. I didn't think much of it because of his generally nonchalant behavior, but I did experience a slight premonition as I parked the car and went around the house to let them out. Scout was agitated, but Boomer still did not get up. He lay in the kennel gasping for breath, and I knew something was badly wrong. As I climbed in to help him, a passing motorist noticed I was having trouble and stopped to help.

I hollered to Nona that Boomer was sick, and she brought the car around so we could take him to the vet. With the help of that Good Samaritan, I managed to lift Boomer up and move him to the car. He died in my arms.

We put Scout in the house and raced Boomer to the vet, but he was gone. We stayed with him awhile, cried over him, and arranged to have his ashes spread in the Hill Country. When we got back to the house, Scout ran down to the kennel looking for him and, not finding him, seemed somehow to realize that he wasn't coming back. I still shiver when I remember how she keened in her grief, voicing what we all felt that terrible day.

Because the two were so attached, I worried that it would take Scout a long time to get over her loss. Actually, I think she got used to being the only dog in the house pretty quickly and enjoyed getting all the attention. By this time, Nona had retired from her job as a schoolteacher, and Scout was not alone all that often. She still loved to go swimming at Redbud Isle and take long walks with us in the neighborhood. She became more protective of us and even a little crotchety, occasionally nipping at other dogs coming into the yard.

I suppose I began to get a little crotchety myself as time passed, and I was determined to spend more time hunting and fishing. Corky and I joined the Bucksnag Hunting Club down in the rice country along the Texas coast

and opened a whole new chapter in our long relationship. The Bucksnag, named for a nearby creek, is an old hotel built at the turn of the last century on the banks of the Colorado River in the heart of one of the biggest rice-producing areas in the world. Sited across from the post office on the main street of the little town of Garwood, the rambling clapboard structure is a classic roadhouse surrounded by porches that give hunters and dogs a place to lounge. In the evenings, wonderful smells emerge from the the kitchen, and the tables are filled with people helping themselves to the traditional fare of the Texas Gulf Coast and savoring their anticipation of the day ahead.

Thanks to the cornucopia of water

and food available in this region of the Texas coast, millions of migratory waterfowl spend the winter there each year; the spectacle of their arrival is one of the greatest outdoor experiences anyone can have.

Those experiences are all the richer because of the lifelong friendships they engender. It was in these rice fields that I came to know one of Texas' greatest sportsmen and conservationists, David Wintermann. He was also one of the finest men I have ever met. Until his death, I had the privilege of opening the Texas teal season with him each year, and I savored the experience of the outdoors, the dogs, and his company. David and his wife, Eula, loved and respected canines more than any two people I have ever met. Their affection for the dogs that lived with them was exceeded only by their devotion to each other. David has been gone for almost a decade, but in his memory I still go to the same blind with his guide on opening day every year.

Mr. Wintermann was one of the founders of the Bucksnag club, one of the reasons Corky and I like the place so much. Corky reminds me of David Wintermann—he knows as much about retrievers as anyone I ever met, and he is truly at home in the marsh. Corky is such a good shot that many times I have put my gun down and just sat back and watched him in admiration. I love to be in the field with him.

Corky also puts up with Scout and me. After Boomer died, I began to take Scout down to the Bucksnag. Although she did not go to the field with us in the mornings, I would wrap her in camouflage and, because dogs were not allowed in the hotel, sneak her upstairs to our bedroom where she would sleep on the floor between Corky and me. Then I would get up really early in the morning, sneak her back downstairs, and let her out so she could hang out with some of the local dogs that seemed always to be around. In the evenings after dinner, we would sit around on the porch with the other hunters and visit, talk about the next morning's hunt, and tell stories about our dogs. Scout would usually curl up next to me with her head on my lap.

That was where she lay at the beginning of the Christmas holidays in her twelfth year—old for a dog. Corky and I had taken her down to the Bucksnag for our last goose hunt of the year and, as usual, planned to spirit her up to our room and leave her in the morning while we went out to the fields. I had promised to take some teenage boys from Houston on their first goose hunt, and Nona had flown up to New Jersey where we planned to spend Christmas with our new grandson, Alexander. The plan was for me to finish the hunt, put Scout in the kennel in Austin, and join the rest of the family for Alexander's first Christmas. The only reason I was still in Texas was that I had made a promise to those kids, and introducing young people to the outdoors is a passion of mine. As I sat there with Scout and Corky, the guides, and my friends, I realized this was the first time in my memory that I was in a hurry to finish the hunt.

The weather looked promising for the next morning, and the guides were sure we would see lots of birds. We all grew excited with anticipation, and noticing how attached I was to Scout, one of the guides said, "Why don't you bring her along?" I explained that although I thought she was highly trained, she had never hunted before. Corky chimed in and reminded me that I had always wanted to see what she could do in a real hunting situation. Soon everyone was encouraging me to bring her along, and though I was reluctant to do so, I gradually convinced myself that she would love it and we would finally have a chance to share the activity for which she was born, bred, and trained. I gave in with some trepidation but also felt excited that we were finally going to hunt together.

The next morning Scout and I got up with the rest of the hunters around 4:30 a.m. There is a lot of activity around the lodge before leaving, as the hunters gather their gear, fortify themselves with coffee, make last-minute plans, and head out to the fields. It is exhilarating, and Scout was into it from the very beginning. Sensing the anticipation, she was ready to go, wagging her tail furiously and looking at me as if to ask, "What's taking you so long?"

In the pitch-black pre-dawn, we rode out to the rice fields with kids and dogs and decoys and all the rest of the trappings of the hunt. As we unloaded the trucks, we could hear the geese on the ponds, waking up with their low chuckling call before they fly, a sound like no other in nature. It was cold and wet, as a waterfowl hunt is supposed to be, and the weather seemed to make it all the more invigorating for Scout. She got acquainted with the other dogs, all of whom were old hands at this hunting business, and they seemed comfortable with having her along.

The first step in a goose hunt is to put out the spread, an array of several hundred plastic windsocks that, when attached to sticks jammed into the ground, resemble a huge flock of geese feeding in the field. This is a method of decoying geese developed in the rice prairies of Texas by legendary guides Marvin Tyler and Jimmy Reel. Reel was another founder of the Bucksnag and is generally credited with inventing the spread, although in the early days they actually used diapers and the method was known as a "rag spread." As I trudged through the muddy field, putting out my decoys, Scout stayed right at my side in the dark.

Daylight arrived with a spectacular sunrise, and we all found our spots amidst the decoys. We were thrilled to have a little breeze, which tends to make the plastic flutter and seem alive, thus increasing the chance of attracting the geese, which, by the time they reach the Texas coast, are pretty wary.

Scout heeled and took her place at my side as the guides began blowing their calls and the geese rose off the pond to move out to the fields for breakfast. It was a wonderful feeling to have her there beside me after all the many hours spent in training, and as she watched the sky with anticipation, I could hardly wait for her first opportunity to bring back a real goose.

In minutes, the red sky was mottled with thousands of birds coming at us in wave after wave. We crouched low to keep from being seen, and Scout seemed to understand as she snuggled tight up against me, concealing herself perfectly. As the great birds approached, I took a shot and missed. Scout seemed okay with that and even looked at me as if I had let her down on her first hunt. I breathed a sigh of relief. Despite her tendency to spook at loud noises, I was sure I had made the right decision to bring her, and we were set for the time of our lives. Corky was close by and watching us carefully. I looked over at him, and he winked at me in reassurance.

Soon the sky was black with skeins of the magnificent birds: snow geese, speckled-bellies, Canadas, and more. I looked back behind me to check on the kids from Houston, and they were appropriately in awe as the sound of the coming birds increased to a roar. Suddenly, the geese were on top of us and everyone started shooting at once. The boys were obviously thrilled and having the time of their lives, which, in turn, thrilled me. I had my dog with me and some great kids were enjoying their first goose hunt. It was turning out to be a wonderful day.

The geese did not stop coming. As more and more birds pulsed toward us in the morning sky, gunfire filled the air with the sound of thunder.

And Scout was gone.

Suddenly, amidst all the excitement,

I was overcome with feelings of terror and loss and guilt. My Scout had disappeared. I ran to find Corky to see if he had seen her, and the two of us began at that moment a search that would go on for the next twenty hours. I couldn't believe I had let this happen and I was physically ill. For hours after the other hunters had left, we walked through the rice fields calling and calling her name. Nothing.

We went back to the Bucksnag and got help from other hunters who searched all afternoon. I went to every farmhouse for miles around and pleaded with the owners to let me know if they had any sign of her. I stopped at every tractor and put my business card on the windshield. I posted rewards in all the nearby towns and visited every little store where I thought the word of my lost dog would spread. The managers let me put notices up among the Christmas decorations and promised to contact me if they received any word of her. Nothing.

There was no sign of her anywhere.

As we searched up and down the back roads and canals of

the rice country, the sounds and symbols of Christmas all around us were lost in a gathering gloom. I called ahead to New Jersey to inform my family of what had happened, and the pall of this catastrophe I had created reached all the way across the country.

At one point, we experienced a flurry of hope and excitement as someone called the Bucksnag, claimed they had found Scout, and wanted to collect the reward. It turned out to be a false hope. I don't know what I would have done had Corky not been there to console me and push forward with the search. Evening came and there was still no sign of her, so I drove my dear friend back up to his farm, turned around in the middle of the night, and went back to the fields to search some more.

I spent the night in a motel on the highway, got up early the next morning, and started all over again, calling and calling her name but there was no sign of her anywhere.

Nothing.

I conjured up all kinds of images of my little companion out there alone with the snakes, coyotes, skunks, and all kinds of wild things that a city dog like Scout would never have experienced. Near panic, I realized I had a reservation to fly to New Jersey the next morning to be with my new grandson. But how could I possibly go with no sign of my dog?

I stayed constantly in touch with Corky, who matter-of-factly told me that at this point she was either going to turn up or she wasn't and not much else I could do would make any difference. Scout was wearing a collar with her name and my home telephone number in Austin, so it was always possible that someone might find her and give me a call. With that glimmer of hope amid a whole lot of dread, I managed to board the plane the next day and head east for Christmas with my family.

I got to New Jersey a week before Christmas and everyone greeted me as if I had been in the hospital or had lost my best friend—which I had. I unpacked my things in a house full of presents and good Christmas smells, and I used my cell phone to call home every half-hour to check for messages, for any sign of Scout. In addition to the terrible guilt I felt about putting Scout in harm's way, I was further depressed that my actions had transformed a family Christmas, which should have been a sensational experience with a new grandchild, to a week of worry about a missing and beloved member of the family.

We tried to break the pall by going to Manhattan for some last-minute shopping. There is no place like New York City at Christmas. The music, the decorations, the chilly air, and the spirit of the season are as powerful on Fifth Avenue as any place on earth. But as I trudged past the magnificent department store windows, the only image I saw in the glass was of Scout wandering around in the prairie back home, facing who knows what obstacles. I went into St. Patrick's Cathedral and prayed that she was safe and that I would see her again.

Back in New Jersey, we sat by the phone and waited. Alexander, who knew Scout as "Woof Woof," was thankfully oblivious to the nagging anxiety that was getting worse for the rest of us. The week went by in a dreamlike state as we exulted in Alexander's every new holiday discovery while at the same time growing sadder with no word of our Scout. It felt as though it couldn't have gotten any better but it also couldn't have gotten any worse—all at the same time. I checked my voice mail and called Corky incessantly. Our friendship of many years continued to deepen as he quietly encouraged me not to give up.

I never did. On Christmas Eve, we were sitting around the kitchen, feeding the baby and preparing food for the next day. The mood was glum. It was too painful to imagine life without Scout, but just as it seemed we might have to, I checked my messages on my home phone in Austin.

Time stood still while I listened to my voicemail. "Well," said a faint female voice, "we've got your little dog down here. She's kinda gray in the face. Has a green collar. It's snowing and we thought you might want to come pick her up." Pandemonium broke loose in the kitchen. Nona had been headed out to the grocery store but raced back into the kitchen as everyone whooped and rejoiced.

Then there was a "click" and the phone went dead.

In stunned silence we all tried to digest what had happened. First of all, it seemed very unlikely that it was snowing in South Texas. Second, we had no idea who or where this woman was and why she had hung up without telling us. Frantically, I called Corky, and, miracle of miracles, he told me that he and his girlfriend had driven from Austin to the coast for Christmas Eve dinner with his mother, and on the way he had gone back to the rice fields to check for the dog. "I'll hang loose here," he said, "while you see if you can figure out where she is. And by the way, it *is* snowing in Texas."

This had to be an omen. Hurrahs went up again in the kitchen, but then we remembered that we still had no idea where Scout was or who had her. At that point, I gained a whole new appreciation for the younger generation as my son, Andrew, as comfortable with technology as he is with his own skin, started punching numbers into my cell phone. He retrieved the number of the lady who had called me, and I called her right back while the rest of the family held their breath.

The first thing she did was apologize for not finishing the call; she explained that she had no money and was calling me on a phone card, which ran out while we were talking. I thanked her about twenty times and asked her where she was. She told me that she was in the little town of Rock Island, Texas, nearly twenty miles north of where Scout had been lost. My dog was headed to Austin; she was going home. The lady, whose name was Maria, said that Scout had actually showed up a couple of days before in the woods near her house trailer but would not come into the yard. It was only when what

turned out to be the heaviest snow in a hundred years began to fall that Maria could coax Scout in from the cold with the promise of shelter and food.

I told Maria that I had a friend nearby who would come pick up Scout. Maria wasn't too sure about giving Scout to a stranger and had me describe Corky and his pickup in detail before she agreed. It turned out Corky was less than fifteen miles from Rock Island, and he headed there immediately. I asked him how much money he had with him, and he and his companion went through their pockets and wallets and purses and came up with about $245. I told them I was good for it if they would give it to Maria. They took a just-opened Christmas card, marked out the names, and addressed it to the lady from me with my thanks and the money.

Corky found the trailer. There were several well-fed dogs in the yard, but Maria's home was another matter. The windows were shattered and covered with cardboard, a broken light bulb hung over the door, and the whole place needed painting. Apparently the one dog she allowed in the house was Scout, who peeked out from behind her legs when Corky went up to the door and introduced himself. Scout was glad to see Corky and came right to him. He handed Maria the secondhand card with her Christmas present inside and suggested she look inside before throwing it into the fire. Scout jumped right up into the truck, and Corky climbed in behind her as Maria opened the card and squealed with surprise. He told me that as they drove away from the trailer, Maria and her roommate stood on the porch and shouted Merry Christmas until the truck was out of sight. They lived so far from the Bucksnag that they hadn't heard about the little lost dog or the reward. They had taken her in simply because they knew she was cold and hungry out in the snow.

Scout was a mess.

She had obviously tangled with a skunk and no telling what else, but because of the heavily falling snow, Corky and his friend let her ride up in the cab with them, pretty much ruining their Christmas Eve clothes. Corky called me in New Jersey when he had her in the truck; he was gasping for breath between laughing and recounting the entire adventure, especially Maria's kindness and delight.

I went to bed that night profoundly moved by the multiple gifts this special Christmas had granted. I got my dog back because of a lady who cared enough to take her in and a lifelong friend who cared enough to bring her home.

Today Corky and I still look forward to our autumn ritual at the marsh. Scout still goes out and gets the paper for me every morning. She is much grayer, particularly in her face, and yet in many ways she seems to have a new lease on life. I wish she could talk and tell me the story because there is a fresh spring in her step and I get the feeling she was transformed in some way by her great adventure. She definitely developed some survival skills; these days, she will not pass a culvert without checking it out or a puddle of water without taking a drink.

I keep her close to me all the time and am very grateful that I can. She is about the best Christmas present I ever received, and I am doubly blessed because she was given to me twice.